Guide to Reading and Writing Korean

LIVING LANGUAGE®

Published in the United States by Living Language, an imprint of Random House, Inc.

www.livinglanguage.com

Editor: Suzanne McQuade
Production Editor: Ciara Robinson
Production Manager: Tom Marshall
Interior Design: Sophie Chin
Production Design: Ann McBride
Illustrations: Sophie Chin

First Edition

ISBN: 978-0-307-97224-8

This book is available at special discounts for bulk purchases for sales promotions or premiums. Special editions, including personalized covers, excerpts of existing books, and corporate imprints, can be created in large quantities for special needs. For more information, write to Special Markets/ Premium Sales, 1745 Broadway, MD 3-1, New York, New York 10019 or e-mail specialmarkets@ randomhouse.com.

PRINTED IN THE UNITED STATES OF AMERICA

10 9 8

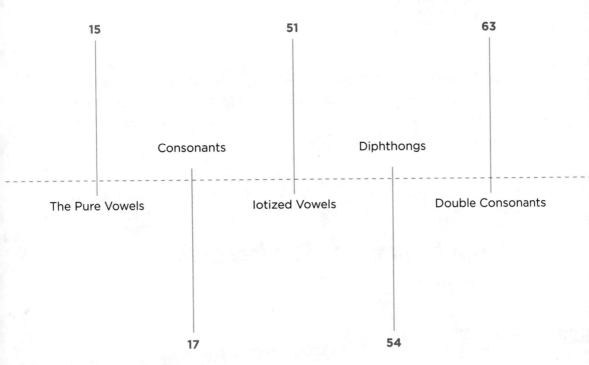
OUTLINE

Part 1: An Introduction to Hangeul

The Korean orthographic system is called Hangeul. Sounds are represented by individual jamo (symbols), and the jamo are combined into syllables. Either two or three jamo can be combined to form a single syllable, on rare occasion, four jamo will be combined in one syllable.

The Korean Alphabet

CONSONANTS	VOWELS
ㄱ giyeok	ㅏ a
ㄲ ssanggiyeok	ㅐ ae
ㄴ nieun	ㅑ ya
ㄷ digeut	ㅒ yae
ㄸ ssangdigeut	ㅓ eo
ㄹ rieul	ㅔ e
ㅁ mieum	ㅕ yeo
ㅂ bieup	ㅖ ye
ㅃ ssangbieup	ㅗ o
ㅅ siot	ㅘ wa
ㅆ ssangsiot	ㅙ wae
ㅇ ieung	ㅚ oe
ㅈ jieut	ㅛ yo

CONSONANTS	VOWELS
ㅉ ssangjieut	ㅜ u
ㅊ chieut	ㅝ wo
ㅋ kieuk	ㅞ we
ㅌ tieut	ㅟ wi
ㅍ pieup	ㅠ yu
ㅎ hieut	ㅡ eu
	ㅢ ui
	ㅣ i

Pronunciation

The consonant characters are said to illustrate the position of the tongue, teeth, and lips when pronouncing that particular letter. Notice how the characters for corresponding voiced (ㄷ *d*) and voiceless (ㅌ *t*) consonants are similar in Hangeul. There are several exceptions to pronunciation rules in Korean; pay close attention to the audio portion of this course so that you learn how to pronounce each word carefully.

Consonants

ㄱ	g	like *g* in *go* when between vowels; sometimes like the *k* in *kept*
ㅋ	k	like *k* in *kept*
ㄴ	n	like *n* in *never*
ㄷ	d	like *t* in *stop* when between vowels; sometimes like the *t* in *tip*

ㅌ	t	like *t* in *tip*
ㄹ	r/l	like *l* in *lip*; between vowels, like *r* in *rail*; at the beginning of words, ㄹ is either unpronounced or pronounced as *n*
ㅅ	s	like *s* in *pass*; when followed by ㅣ, like *sh* in *she*
ㅈ	j	like *j* in *jump* when between vowels; sometimes like *ch* in *check*
ㅊ	ch	like *ch* in *check*
ㅁ	m	like *m* in *mother*
ㅂ	b	like *b* in *boy* when between vowels; sometimes like *p* in *pick*
ㅍ	p	like *p* in *pick*
ㅇ	-/-ng	The zero initial is used in syllables that begin with a vowel sound. When it follows a vowel at the end of a syllable, it is pronounced *ng* (ex. 안 = an; 녕 = nyeong)

ㅎ	h	like English h in hot; when appearing after ㄱ, ㄷ, ㅂ, ㅅ, ㅈ, or ㅊ, it is not pronounced, but instead aspirates the following consonant: ㄱ (k), ㄷ (t), ㅂ (p), ㅅ (t), ㅈ (ch), or ㅊ (t)

Double Consonants

ㄲ	gg/kk	like k in kept but tensed
ㄸ	dd/tt	like t in stop but tensed
ㅃ	bb/pp	like p in picture but tensed
ㅆ	ss	like s in spit but tensed; when followed by ㅣ, somewhere between sh in she and c in cease, but tensed
ㅉ	jj	like j in jump but tensed

Vocalics
PURE VOWELS

ㅗ	o	like English o in so
ㅓ	eo	like the u in cup
ㅏ	a	like the a in father
ㅣ	i	like the ee in feet

ㅜ	u	like the *oo* in *coop*
ㅡ	eu	like the *i* in *bid*, but pronounced further back in the throat

IOTIZED VOWELS

ㅛ	yo	like English *yo* in *yo-yo*
ㅕ	yeo	like the *you* in *young*
ㅑ	ya	like the *ya* in *yacht*
ㅠ	yu	like the *you* in *youth*

DIPHTHONGS

ㅐ	ae	like the *e* in *set*
ㅒ	yae	like *yet* without the *t*
ㅔ	e	like the *a* in *take*
ㅖ	ye	like *yay*
ㅘ	wa	like the *wa* in *water*
ㅙ	wae	like the *we* in *wet*
ㅚ	oe	like the *oy* in *boy*
ㅝ	wo	like the *wha* in *what*
ㅞ	we	like *we* in *weigh*
ㅟ	wi	like the *whea* in *wheat*
ㅢ	ui	similar to *we*

Liaison

Korean has rules of liaison, which state that when certain sounds are combined, some of them will change to become new sounds. This happens in other languages as well; think of the difference in English between *rate* and *rated*: the t sound changes to a d sound before *–ed*, even though the spelling is unchanged. This is very similar to the Korean rules of liaison, which are as follows:

ㄱ, ㄷ, AND ㅂ

Whenever you see ㄱ (g, k), ㄷ (d, t), or ㅂ (b, p) before ㄹ (l), ㅁ (m), or ㄴ (n) they are pronounced ㅇ (ng), ㅁ (m), and ㄴ (n) respectively. The ㄹ (l), if following any of the three above, also changes to an ㄴ (n) sound through this liaison.

습 + 니 = 습니
seup + ni = seumni

고맙습니다.
Gomapseumnida.
Thank you.

ㄹ

When ㄹ (l) follows any consonant apart from ㄹ (l) or ㄴ (n), it is pronounced (n). When ㄹ (l) and ㄴ (n) are together in any combination (ㄹ+ㄴ/ㄴ+ㄹ), they are pronounced as (ll).

CONSONANT ENDINGS

Any word ending in a consonant and not followed by a particle will swallow the final consonant. This means that you will begin to pronounce the sound, but not completely pronounce it.

ㅊ (ch), ㅈ (j), ㅅ (s), ㅆ (ss), and ㅎ (h)

When any of these consonants appear at the end of the word, they are swallowed as above, but the beginning of the sound you produce will be the beginning of a ㄷ (d, t) sound.

How Hangeul Works

Let's start to look at how these individual letters combine to form syllables.

ㅇ + ㅏ + ㄴ = 안
- + a + n = an

ㄴ + ㅕ + ㅇ = 녕
n + yeo + ng = nyeong

ㅎ + ㅏ = 하
h + a = ha

ㅅ + ㅔ = 세
s + e = se

ㅇ + ㅛ = 요
- + yo = yo

You will learn more about the positioning of individiual jamo within the syllable (especially how vowels affect the positioning) as you learn to write each letter in Part 2.

Now let's look at how these syllables combine to form words and phrases.

안 + 녕 + 하 + 세 + 요 = 안녕하세요?
An + nyeong + ha + se + yo = Annyeonghaseyo?
How are you?

Again:

ㄱ + ㅗ = 고
g + o = go

ㅁ + ㅏ + ㅂ = 맙
m + a + p = map

ㅅ + ㅡ + ㅂ = 습
s + eu + p = seup

ㄴ + ㅣ = 니
n + i = ni

ㄷ + ㅏ = 다
d + a = da

고 + 맙 + 습 + 니 + 다 = 고맙습니다.
Go + map + seup + ni + da = Gomapseumnida.*
Thank you. (deferential)

*Notice the rule of liaison at work in this expression.

Punctuation

Korean writing used to be written top to bottom following the Chinese writing
style. In modern times, the direction of Korean writing became similar to the
western style: Korean text is written and read from left to right on the page, and
each sentence uses punctuation marks just as in English.

좋은 하루 되세요.

Joeun haru dueseyo.

Have a good day.

잘 지내세요?

Jal jinaeseyo?

How are you doing? (lit: *Are you spending time well?*)

In addition to periods and question marks, Korean writing uses commas and exclamation marks as well.

만나서 반갑습니다!

Mannaseo bangapseumnida!

Glad to see you!

리사 씨, 만나서 반갑습니다.

Lisassi, mannaseo bangapseumnida.

Ms. Lisa, I'm glad to see you.

Colons (:) and semi-colons (;), however, are not used in Korean writing the same way they are used in English, so it's best to avoid using them for now.

Part 2: Study and Practice

Let's study the letters of the Korean alphabet progressively to help you commit them to memory and practice using them in writing. We'll start by looking at some basic vowels and consonants and having you start building words using only what you've learned. We'll then continue to build on these until you have the entire alphabet down. We'll also show you how each letter and syllable looks handwritten, and show a few examples of written syllables and words for each letter.

Let's start with the pure vowels.

The Pure Vowels

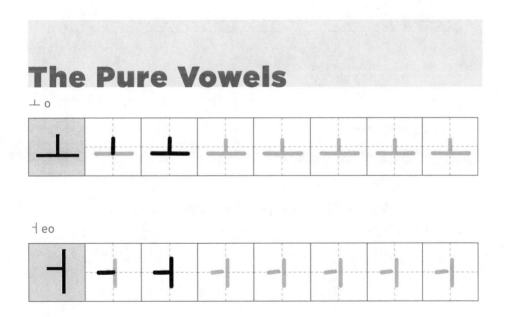

ㅗ o

ㅓ eo

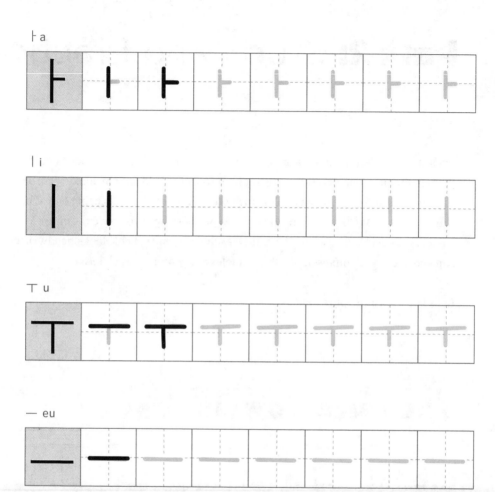

Practice writing these vowels until you have them down. Now let's add consonants in groups.

Consonants

Group 1: ㅇ and ㅎ

ㅇ −/−ng

ㅎ h

In Korean, every syllable contains at least one consonant and one vowel. When vowels occur in a syllable of their own, they will appear following ㅇ. Let's see how this looks with the pure vowels.

오 o

어 eo

아 a

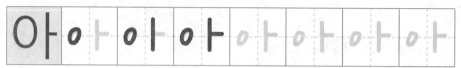

이 i

우 u

으 eu

It's easiest to remember when combining syllables that the consonant appears on top of ㅗ o, ㅜ u, and — eu because they are horizontal, while the consonant will appear next to the vertical ㅓ eo, ㅏ a, and ㅣ i. This means you can read the syllable left to right or top to bottom.

Now trying using the pure vowels with ㅎ:

호 ho

허 heo

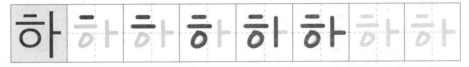

하 ha

히 hi

후 hu

흐 heu

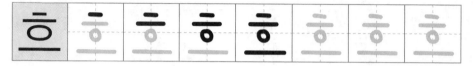

Now practice writing the following in Korean:

오이 oi

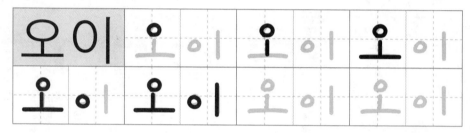

아이 ai

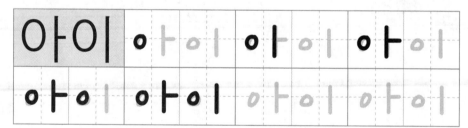

어항 eohang

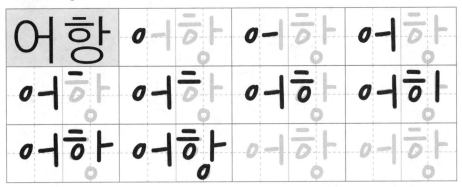

Group 2: ㄱ, ㅋ, and ㄴ

ㄱ g

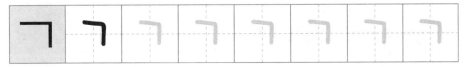

ㅋ k

ㄴ n

Let's see how these look with the pure vowels in syllables:

고 go

거 geo

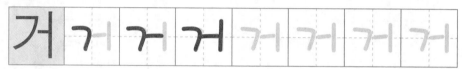

가 ga

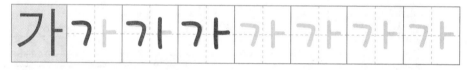

기 gi

구 gu

그 geu

코 ko

커 keo

카 ka

키 ki

쿠 ku

크 keu

노 no

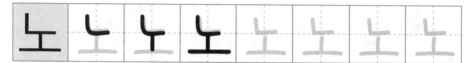

너 neo

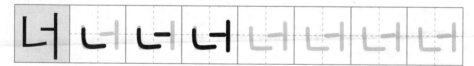

나 na

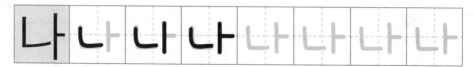

니 ni

ㅜ nu

ㅡ neu

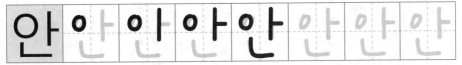

Remember that three letters are also often combined into one syllable. In these instances, the consonant will appear on top of the horizontal ㅗ o, ㅜ u, and ㅡ eu and next to the vertical ㅓ eo, ㅏ a, and ㅣ i, even when followed by another consonant. This means you should read the syllable left to right, then top to bottom.

Let's look at some three letter syllables, noting the position of the consonants and vowels in each:

안 an

은 eun

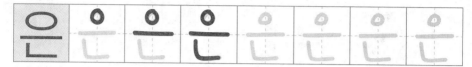

는 neun

각 gak

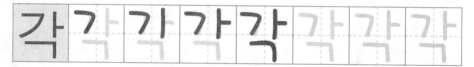

And using the two letters you already know:

한 han

학 hak

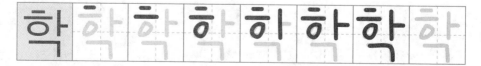

운 un

얼 eok

혼 hon

은 eun

깅 ging

혹 hok

농 nong

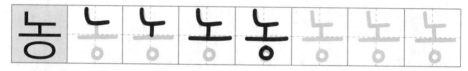

하고 hago

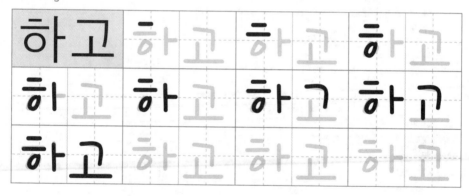

Notice in the final example that there are two syllables, each with its own vowel. You will occasionally see four letters in a syllable (괜찮아요 gwaenchanhayo *it's all right*); these four-letter syllables will also be read left to right then top to bottom.

Let's look at a few more examples showing how words with multiple syllables are written.

언니 eonni (*female's older sister*)

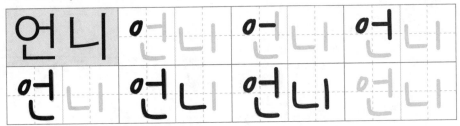

누나 nuna (*male's older sister*)

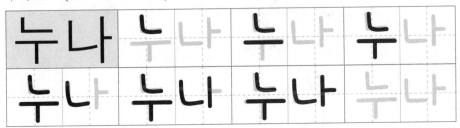

쿠키 kuki (*cookie*)

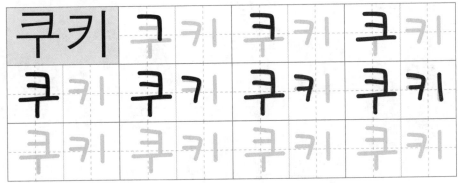

Now practice writing the following words in Korean:

한국 hankook (*Korea*)

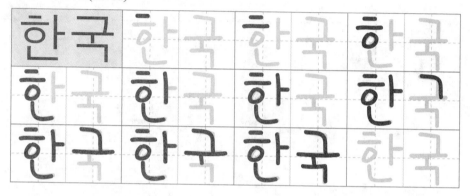

악기 akki (*musical instrument*)

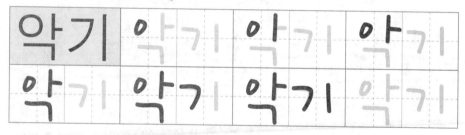

가구 kaku (*furniture*)

Write out the Hangeul for each transcribed word below. Since ㄱ is often transcribed as k, we'll use an underlined k̲ to indicate the places you should use ㅋ.

1. nun (*eye*)

_____

2. nongku (*basketball*)

_____

3. hongk̲ong (*Hong Kong*)

_____

4. nai (*age*)

_____

5. kukeo (*native language*)

_____

ANSWER KEY
1. 눈 2. 농구 3. 홍콩 4. 나이 5. 국어

Group 3: ㄷ, ㅌ, and ㄹ

ㄷ d

ㅌ t

ㄹ r/l

Let's see how these look with the pure vowels in syllables:

도 do

더 deo

다 da

디 di

두 du

드 deu

토 to

터 teo

타 ta

티 ti

투 tu

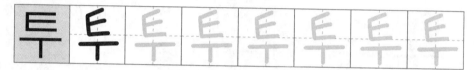

트 teu

로 no

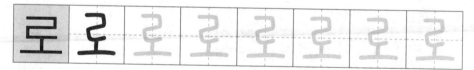

러 neo

라 na

리 ni

루 nu

르 neu

Now practice writing the following in Korean:

하루 haru (*day*)

한글 Hangeul (*Korean alphabet*)

라디오 radio (*radio*)

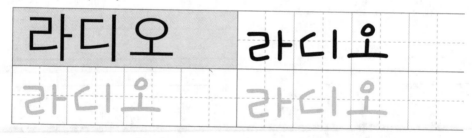

할인 halin (*discount*)

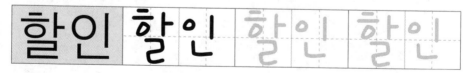

기타 kita (*guitar*)

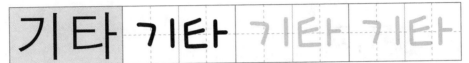

Write out the Hangeul for each transcribed word below.

1. dolaoda (*to return*)

_____

2. nohda (*to put*)

_____

3. dokil (*Germany*)

_____

4. takku (*ping-pong*)

_____

5. hana (*one*)

_____

ANSWER KEY
1. 돌아오다 2. 놓다 3. 독일 4. 탁구 5. 하나

Group 4: ㅅ, ㅈ, and ㅊ

ㅅ s

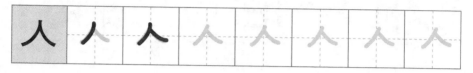

ㅈ j

ㅊ ch

Let's see how these look with the pure vowels in syllables:

소 so

서 seo

사 sa

시 si

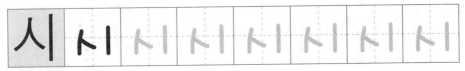

수 su

스 seu

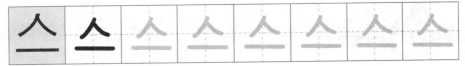

조 jo

저 jeo

자 ja

지 ji

주 ju

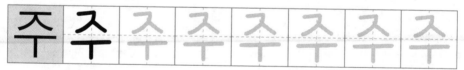

즈 jeu

초 cho

처 cheo

차 cha

치 chi

추 chu

츠 cheu

Now practice writing the following in Korean:

잘 jal (*well*)

가족 gajok (*family*)

천천히 cheoncheonhi (*slowly*)

사전 sajeon (*dictionary*)

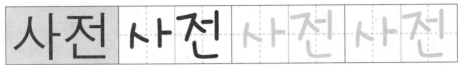

식당 sikdang (*restaurant*)

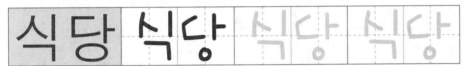

조카 joka (*nephew/niece*)

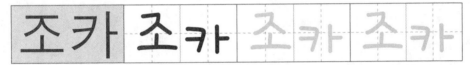

Write out the Hangeul for each transcribed word below.

1. jihacheol (*subway*)

_____

2. jadongcha (*car*)

_____

3. saramdeuli (*people* + subject particle)

_____

4. jungkuk *(China)*

_____

5. jongi *(paper)*

_____

ANSWER KEY
1. 지하철 2. 자동차 3. 사람들이 4. 중국 5. 종이

Group 5: ㅁ, ㅂ, and ㅍ

ㅁ m

ㅂ b

ㅍ p

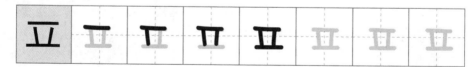

Let's see how these look with the pure vowels in syllables:

모 mo

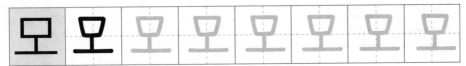

머 meo

마 ma

미 mi

무 mu

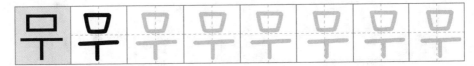

므 meu

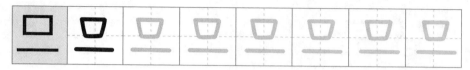

보 bo

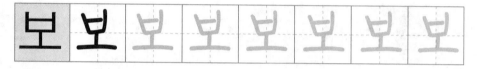

버 beo

바 ba

비 bi

부 bu

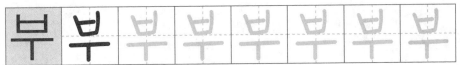

브 beu

포 po

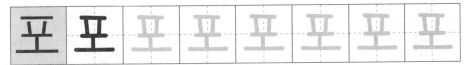

퍼 peo

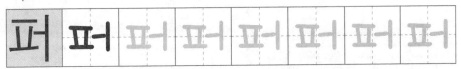

파 pa

피 pi

푸 pu

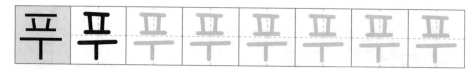

프 peu

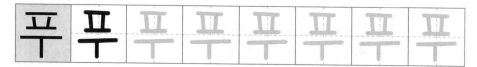

Now practice writing the following in Korean:

어머니 eomeoni (*mother*)

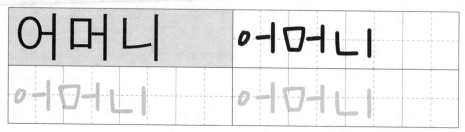

아버지 abeoji (*father*)

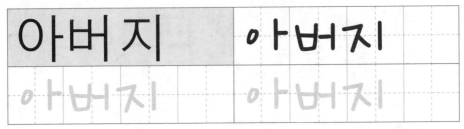

다시 한번 dashi hanbeon (*one more time*)

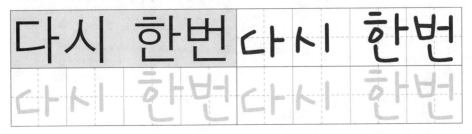

감사합니다 Kamsahamnida. (*Thank you.*)

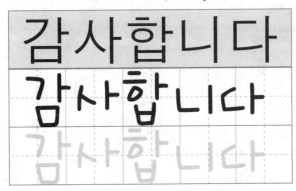

프랑스어 peurangseueo (*French language*)

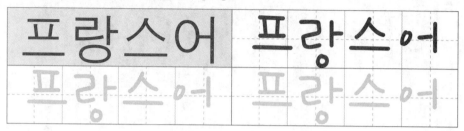

Write out the Hangeul for each transcribed word below.

1. sungham (*name,* honorific)

   _____

2. eumakeul deudda (*to listen to music*)

   _____

3. hankukeoleul kongbuhada (*to study Korean*)

   _____

4. ibhakhada (*to enroll in school*)

   _____

5. keuleohjiman (*however*)

   _____

ANSWER KEY
1. 성함 2. 음악을 듣다 3. 한국어를 공부하다 4. 입학하다 5. 그렇지만

Iotized Vowels

Let's add some more vowels.

ㅛ yo

ㅕ yeo

ㅑ ya

ㅠ yu

Note that these vowels look similar to their corresponding pure vowels, with an extra stroke added to them.

ㅛ	yo	ㅗ	o
ㅕ	yeo	ㅓ	eo
ㅑ	ya	ㅏ	a
ㅠ	yu	ㅜ	u

Now practice writing the following in Korean:

학교 hakkyo (*school*)

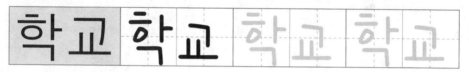

영어 yeongeo (*English*)

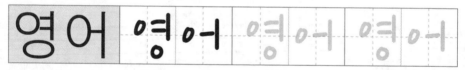

저녁 jeonyeok (*evening/ dinner*)

하얀 hayan (*white*)

우유 uyu (*milk*)

Write out the Hangeul for each transcribed word below. Since ㄱ is often transcribed as k, we'll use an underlined k̲ to indicate the places you should use ㅋ.

1. k̲eompyuteo (*computer*)

_____

2. toyoil (*Saturday*)

_____

3. kakyeok (*price*)

_____

4. jaknyeon (*last year*)

_____

5. yangmal (*socks*)

_____

ANSWER KEY
1. 컴퓨터 2. 토요일 3. 가격 4. 작년 5. 양말

Diphthongs

Diphthongs are combinations of two or more vowels. In Korean, these are considered separate letters of the alphabet. Knowing their base pure vowels will simply help you remember them better. ㅐ ae, for example, is a combination of ㅏ a and ㅣ i (ㅒ yae is its iotized form: note the extra line); ㅙ wae is a combination of ㅗ o, ㅏ a, and ㅣ i.

Diphthong Group 1

ㅐ ae

ㅒ yae

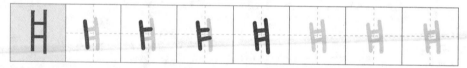

ㅔ e

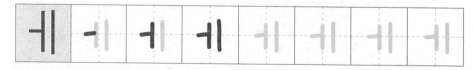

ㅖ ye

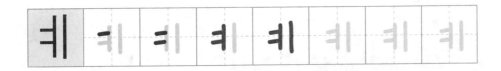

Now practice writing the following in Korean:

책 chaek (*book*)

얘기 yaeki (*story/talk*)

펜 pen (*pen*)

세 se (*age*, honorific)

시계 sikye (*clock*)

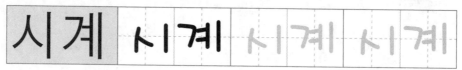

넷 net (*four*)

Write out the Hangeul for each transcribed word below.

1. hayaeyo (*to be white* + polite ending)

_____

2. kyesida (*to be,* honorific)

_____

3. gedaka (*besides/moreover*)

_____

4. eunhaeng (*bank*)

_____

5. nektai (*tie*)

_____

ANSWER KEY
1. 하얘요 2. 계시다 3. 게다가 4. 은행 5. 넥타이

Diphthong Group 2

ㅘ wa

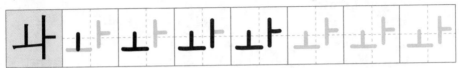

ㅙ wae

ㅚ oe

Keep in mind that syllables using the diphthongs ㅘ wa, ㅙ wae, ㅚ oe will be read consonant-diphthong-consonant; in other words, instead of reading left to right then top to bottom, you will read top to bottom, left to right, then top to bottom again, as in the syllable 화 hwa.

Now practice writing the following in Korean:

화장실 hwajangsil (*bathroom*)

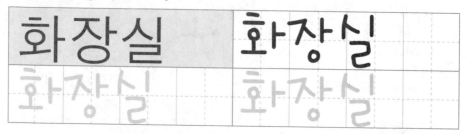

왼쪽 oenjjok (*left*)

괜찮다 kwaenchanda (*to be fine*)

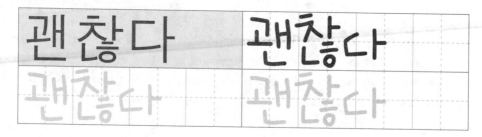

외할머니 oehalmeoni (*maternal grandmother*)

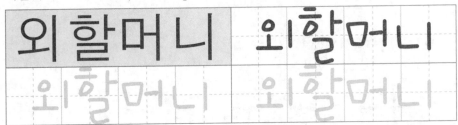

왜 wae (*why*)

Write out the Hangeul for each transcribed word below.

1. hoesa (*company*)

_____

2. sakwa (*apple*)

_____

3. doenjang (*soybean paste*)

_____

4. dwaeji (*pig*)

_____

5. eomeoniwaabeoji (*mother and father*)

_____

Diphthong Group 3

ㅝ wo

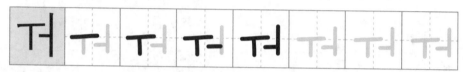

ㅞ we

ㅟ wi

ㅢ ui

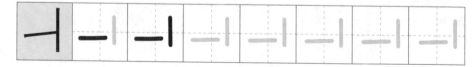

Keep in mind that syllables using the diphthongs ㅝ wo, ㅞ we, ㅟ wi, ㅢ ui will be read consonant-diphthong-consonant; in other words, instead of reading left to right then top to bottom, you will read top to bottom, left to right, then top to bottom again, as in the syllable 권 gwon.

Now practice writing the following in Korean:

배워요 bawoyo (*to learn* + polite ending)

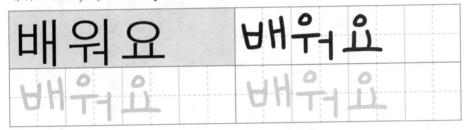

의자 uija (*chair*)

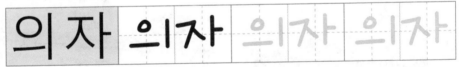

쉬다 swida (*to rest*)

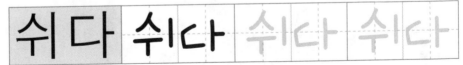

쉽다 swipda (*to be easy*)

웬일인지 wenilinji (*for some reason*)

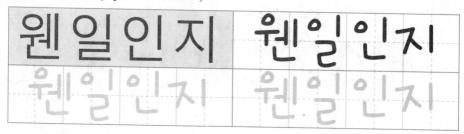

Write out the Hangeul for each transcribed word below.

1. kwi (*ear*)

_____

2. weiteo (*waiter*)

_____

3. webdijaineo (*web designer*)

_____

4. uisa (*doctor*)

_____

5. wolyoil (*Monday*)

_____

Double Consonants

Finally, let's look at Double Consonants.

ㄲ gg/kk

ㄸ dd/tt

ㅃ bb/pp

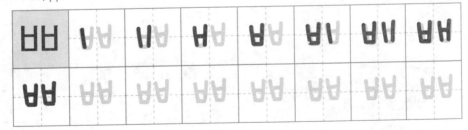

ㅆ ss

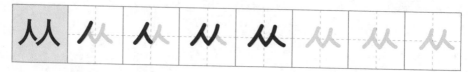

ㅉ jj

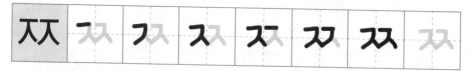

Now practice writing the following in Korean:

바쁘다 babbda (*to be busy*)

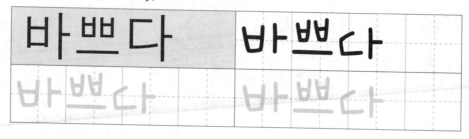

오른쪽 oleunjjok (*right*)

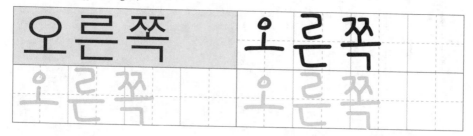

빨간색 ppalgansaek (*red color*)

꽃 kkod (*flower*)

쓴 sseun (*bitter*)

Write out the Hangeul for each transcribed word below.

1. jjan (*salty*)

_____

2. ttal (*daughter*)

_____

3. ssada (*to be cheap*)

_____

4. ttatteuhan (*warm*)

_____

5. annyeonghasimnikka (*Hello/How are you?*, deferential ending)

_____

ANSWER KEY
1. 짠 2. 딸 3. 싸다 4. 따뜻한 5. 안녕하십니까?

Character Practice